Our Lives, Our World

Denmark

Chrysalis Children's Books

First published in the UK in 2005 by
Chrysalis Children's Books
An imprint of Chrysalis Books Group
The Chrysalis Building, Bramley Road
London W10 6SP

Copyright © Chrysalis Books Group Plc 2005
Photography © Kristian Buus, Lene Esthave
and Toke Hage 2005

Compiled and edited by Susie Brooks
Associate Publisher: Joyce Bentley
Designed by: Tall Tree Books Ltd
Photographic consultant: Jenny Matthews
Photographic co-ordinator: Kristian Buus
Picture researcher: Miguel Lamas
Translator: Kristian Buus

ISBN 1 84458 442 9

Printed in China

10 9 8 7 6 5 4 3 2 1

British Library Cataloguing in Publication Data for
this book is available from the British Library.

The Publishers would like to thank the
photographers, Kristian Buus, Lene Esthave and
Toke Hage, for capturing these wonderful children
on film. Many thanks also to Kristian for his support
and encouragement throughout the project.

Corbis: Ray Juno 4(BR), Bob Krist 5(CL); Courtesy of
Danmarks Nationalbank 22(BL); photolibrary.com 5(TL);
Rex Features: David Cole Front Cover(BL), 1(BC), 5(B);
Courtesy of Visit Denmark.com: ©J. Buusman 30(TR).

All reasonable efforts have been made to ensure the reproduction
of content has been done with the consent of copyright owner.
If you are aware of any unintentional omissions please contact
the publishers directly so that any necessary corrections may
be made for future editions.

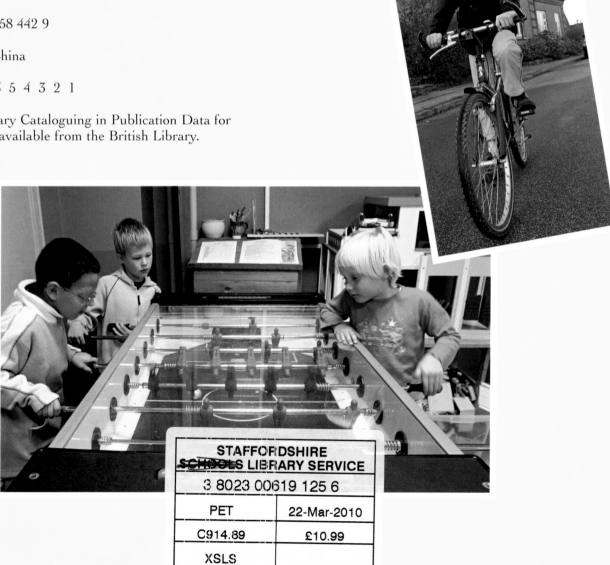

Contents

Hej! – Hello!

We are the children of Denmark and we can't wait to share our lives with you in this book!

Welcome to Denmark!

We've got so much to show you! Let's start by telling you a bit about our country. We hope you'll come and see Denmark for yourself some time soon!

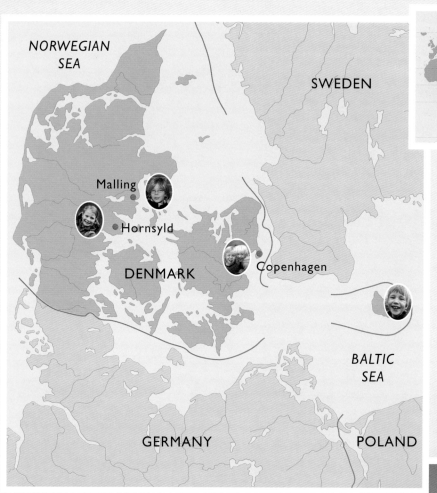

Our country

Denmark is in northern Europe. It is part of an area known as Scandinavia, which also includes Norway, Sweden and Iceland. Sea surrounds most of Denmark. Our country is made up of more than 400 islands as well as the mainland.

Our capital

Copenhagen is our capital city. The Queen of Denmark lives there. She is also Queen of Greenland and the Faroe Islands. Seen here is the Danish Parliament building.

Land and climate

The land in Denmark is mostly low and flat. Inland it is very green, while along the coasts there are huge sandy beaches. The climate is mild – winters are not too cold and summers are not too hot. It can be wet and windy, but the sea breeze is great for watersports!

Tourist spot

There are lots of exciting places to visit in Denmark. Legoland is one of the most famous – the Danes invented lego!

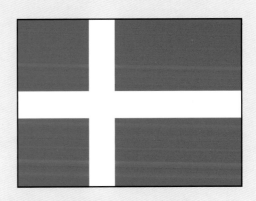

Our flag

Denmark's flag is the oldest national flag in the world.

Speak Danish!

hej – hello/hi

vi ses/farvel – goodbye

vær så venlig [vaer-so-venlie] – please

tak – thank you

National bird

Our national bird is the mute swan. We have lots of water birds and animals in Denmark.

Karina

Hi! My name is Karina Asmussen and I am 9 years old. I live with my mum, dad and two big brothers in Hornsyld on the mainland of Denmark. My cheeky pet dog is called Tessi. She's nearly two years old and she's very playful!

"The most exciting place I've been to is Legoland – they have a great rollercoaster!"

Here we are outside our house. My 20-year-old brother Denni is away at the moment. He's training to be a plumber. Next to me here is Daniel – he's 17 and he's a carpenter.

We have a chicken coop in the garden – I like going out to collect the eggs.

This is the office where dad goes to work. He sells medicine on the internet. Mum works at home, looking after a group of small children.

Dad drives me to school on his way to work. We put my bike in the back of the car so I can cycle home. School starts at 8.00am.

My favourite lessons are art and music because they're the most fun. Here I'm drawing a picture to illustrate the Bible story my teacher is reading.

There are 19 children in my class. At break time I like playing this board game, called Kalaha, with some of the girls. I usually win!

We finish school at 11.30am on Mondays and 12.40pm during the rest of the week. I say goodbye to my best friend Laerke...

...and then I pedal home! It's only a five-minute ride. I carry my books for homework in a rucksack on my back.

"I'm not allowed to ride my bike without a helmet."

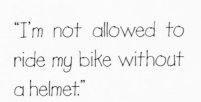

At weekends I love being outside – especially riding my motocross bike!

"My friends say I'm sweet, good and tough!"

I also like running
around with Tessi...

...and making waffles for my tea!

How I make waffles

I mix together some flour, baking powder, sugar and a pinch of salt. I beat in some milk, egg yolks and melted butter. Mum helps me cook the batter on a hot waffle iron.

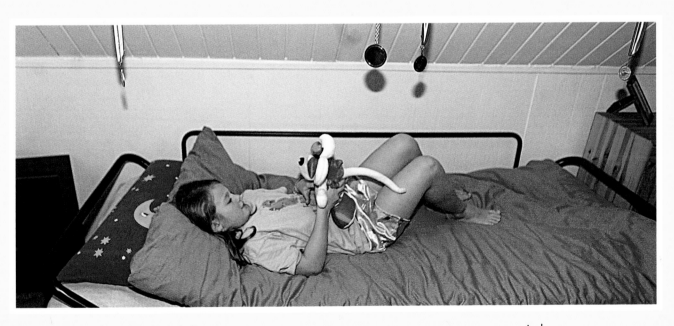

I have to be in bed by 9.30pm. In my room are some medals
I've won for playing football – another of my favourite hobbies!

11

Rasmus

Hello, I'm Rasmus Bille Brahe and I'm 7 years old. I live with my family on the island of Bornholm in the Baltic Sea. We moved here two years ago. It's quite a long way from the rest of Denmark but we can get around by plane or ferry.

"When I grow up I want to be an astronaut – I think it would be really funny to go into space!!"

This is my family! I have a sister, Sidse, who's 4 years old, and a baby brother called Johan. Mum is a teacher and dad works here at home, designing websites.

We live on a farm, way out in the countryside. The postman leaves our mail by the sign to our house and we walk down to pick it up.

Here I am feeding Lille Miv, one of our pet cats - we have six cats altogether! We also have two dogs, a few chickens, some sheep and a duck.

This is the view from our house – it's just been raining! On the land there is a forest, a stream and a small lake. There are lots of little birds around – some of them come to feed on our bird table.

Farming country

Three-quarters of Denmark is covered in farmland. The main crops are cereals, like wheat and barley. Dairy farming is very common too, so there is a lot of grass for grazing cows. Many people farm part-time, or as a hobby, and earn their living by doing other jobs.

I love it when dad lets us ride on the trailer around the farm!

Our sheep have been grazing in the neighbours' field so we're herding them back home.

We return them safely, just as the light fades. In winter here it is dark by 3.00 or 4.00pm!

Back inside, we have a big play fight – then we cuddle up on the sofa for a rest. I go to bed at 8.00pm, but I'm allowed to stay up later on Fridays and Saturdays.

I go to school every morning from Monday to Friday. This is the sign on my classroom door – it says 'Welcome', and all our names are written on it. I am in class OA.

These are some of my classmates!

School years

Rasmus goes to pre-school, but he will soon move up to Grade 1. All children in Denmark have to go to school from the age of 7 until they are 16 (Grade 9). Pre-school and Grade 10 are optional. Lessons are in Danish, but everyone learns English from Grade 4 upwards.

Friday is mostly play day. My best friend Tobias and I are excited because we've just won a game called Star of Africa!

At break time we go to get our milk and lunch packs. Tobias and I play games on the way!

Today's lunch is rye bread with ham and liver pâté, a sausage roll, a raw carrot, sliced apple and some cookies.

Black bread

Dark bread made from rye flour is very common in Denmark. It is often eaten as an open sandwich, called a 'smørrebrød' [*smoerr-broeth*]. Toppings include ham, cheese, pâté and fish.

At home my favourite foods are spare ribs and meatballs. I also love pancakes and homemade elderflower juice – we sometimes have these when friends come for tea!

Millie and Sofia

Hej! We are Millie and Sofia Ramsgaard Skou – we are twins and we're 6 years old. Our mum and dad are divorced but they both live in Copenhagen, so we have two great homes! In both places we share a room with a bunk bed.

Millie

Sofia

"Our friends say we're really sweet. We get told off if we fight or scream or stamp like elephants!"

Here we are eating dinner with Dad and his girlfriend Kaisa. They have a baby called Olivia – our half sister.

This is us leaving for school with mum (her name's Lisbeth) in the courtyard outside her block of flats.

It's fun having a twin! We do lots of things together, like dancing to our favourite pop music...

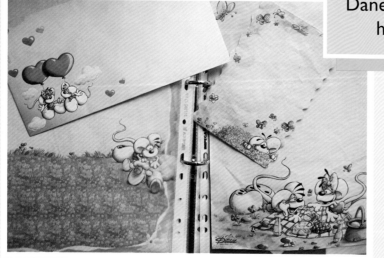

...reading Danish stories...

Hans Christian Anderson

The famous author Hans Christian Anderson came from Denmark. He wrote hundreds of stories including *The Ugly Duckling*, *The Emperor's New Clothes* and *The Little Mermaid*. He died in 1875, but the Danes still celebrate his birthday and his home is now a popular museum.

...and collecting Diddls! Diddls are the cute little characters on our cards and notepaper – we swap them with our friends. You can never have enough Diddls!

Every afternoon we go to after-school club. There are loads of activities. I love table football...

...and I like playing shops. We're selling a sticky cake made from sand and leaves – yum!

I made this bowl in the pottery room!

Sometimes we go shopping in town. Dad takes us in his bicycle cart – it's so exciting when he pedals fast!

Cycling city

Lots of families in Copenhagen use bicycle carts for taking children to school or to the shops. Cycling is the most popular way of getting around town. You can even pay to borrow a bike from a street stand, then get your money back when you return it.

The supermarket sells loads of fun things, including toys. We wish we could get more Diddls!

The money we spend in Denmark is called Krone. Every week we each get 20 Krone (nearly £2) for pocket money.

Famous foods

Denmark has lots of pig farms, so pork is by far the most popular meat. People eat it roasted, in meatballs, in a wide variety of sausages, as hams, salamis and as bacon. Sweet, sticky Danish pastries (called 'wienerbrød' [viener-broeth] in Denmark) are famous all over the world.

Today we're just shopping for food. I help to weigh the broccoli.

In the butcher's there are all sorts of delicious meats to choose from.

For a treat, we stop at the bakery to get some pastries and cakes!

"My favourite foods are Danish sausages and meatballs!" [Millie]

Nichlas

Hi, I'm Nichlas Nielsen Broch-Lips and I'm 9 years old. I live with my mum, dad, brother and sister in Malling, on the eastern side of Denmark's mainland. We have two pet cats called Lakrids (meaning Liquorice) and Killing (Kitten)!

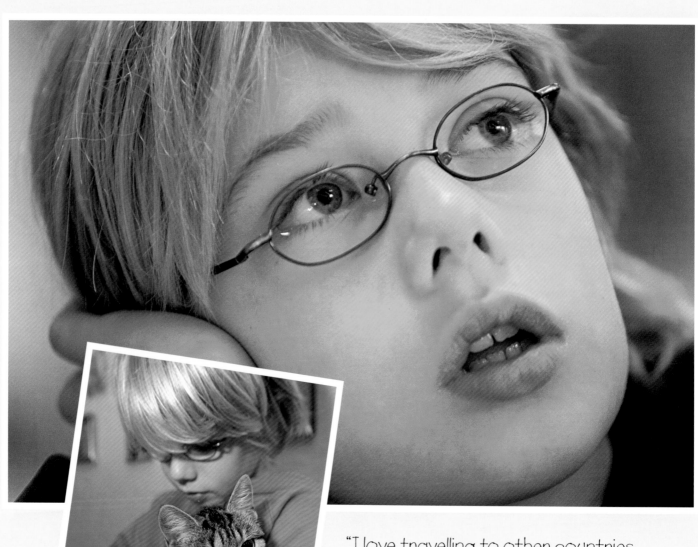

"I love travelling to other countries. My favourite place is Austria, where my mum was born."

Meet my family! My brother Mikkel is 6 years old and my sister Signe Ingrid is 3. Mum works in a shop that sells wooden toys and woolly clothes, and dad is a social worker.

Cosy homes

Like the majority of people in Denmark, Nichlas's family have a comfortable home. Cosy times indoors with family and friends are an important part of Danish life – especially during the long, dark winters!

This is our house. The middle window on the top floor is my bedroom. In the garden is an old water tower. A famous Danish comedian used to own it – he made children's TV programmes there!

The sign reads:
- Skolens kontor
- Malling ungdomsskole
- Skolefritidsordning
- Festsal
- Omklædning - Idræt
- Vareindlevering
- Parkering

VIBART

My school is in Malling, not far away from our house. It takes me about 5 minutes to cycle there. Lessons start at 8.15am – my favourite class is swimming, but I really like all my subjects!

"Our school is huge – there are 600 pupils and 45 teachers!"

Travelling around

People try not to use cars in Denmark, to avoid harming the environment. Like Nichlas, many children cycle to school, and most Danish people own a bike. There are also good bus and train services. Bridges join the different islands and there are ferry links, too.

These are two of my best friends, Søren and Aksel. We think we look cool in this picture!

After school we go to the daycare centre to play while our mums and dads are still at work. I love the Moon Cars!

When I get home I have to do some homework. I'm pretty quick, so it usually takes me less than half an hour.

My favourite hobby is football. I'm a member of a local club called BMI. In the winter I play indoors, once a week. In the summer I play outside more often. I'm usually the goalkeeper.

Popular sports

Sport is very important in Denmark as a way of keeping fit, meeting new friends and having fun. Football, badminton, swimming and handball (like football, but played with the hand and a small ball) are all very popular. Because no one is far from the sea, lots of people also enjoy watersports such as windsurfing and canoeing.

I do press-ups to help keep myself fit and strong!

I also like playing football games on my parents' computer. That's when they're not using it for work or writing emails!

On my bedroom wall I have football posters. I want to play for a professional team when I grow up. These are some of the medals I've won already.

My other hobby is drumming. I've been playing for two years and I'm crazy about it! We have a small studio at home where I can practise. I'm really into rock music – Linkin Park is my favourite band.

Our Year

Here are some important events in our calendar!

JANUARY

New Year's Day At the stroke of midnight people welcome the new year with drinks and almond ring cakes.

FEBRUARY

Fastelavn Children dress up and go round local houses asking for treats. There is a game where we beat a big barrel with a stick until it breaks and sweets fall out!

MARCH/APRIL

Nichlas's birthday: 11th April

Easter We have a special family meal and decorate the table with daffodils, yellow and purple napkins and coloured eggs. People give each other chocolate easter eggs.

Easter school holiday: March/April

Queen Margrethe's birthday We fly flags all around the country to congratulate the queen.

MAY

Great Prayer Day A national holiday when some people go to church and we traditionally eat hot wheat muffins.

Mother's Day We thank our mums for looking after us and give them cards and flowers.

Whitsun A religious festival and also the start of spring. We go outside with picnics and watch the sun dance in the sky!

JUNE

Constitution Day A national holiday when we all fly Danish flags.
Midsummer We light bonfires, have picnics and sing songs.

JULY/AUGUST

Music festivals are held around the country, with all sorts of styles including jazz, rock, pop and folk.

Karina's birthday: 18th July

Summer school holiday: July/August

SEPTEMBER

Rasmus's birthday: 17th September

Arhus festival The eastern city of Arhus hosts music and drama shows and also a Viking festival.

OCTOBER/NOVEMBER

There are film festivals in many parts of the country.

DECEMBER

Christmas Eve We fly flags and have a special evening meal with roast goose and Danish pastries.

Christmas school holiday: December/ January

Christmas Day We open the presents that are piled under our Christmas trees!

Millie & Sofia's birthday: 2nd December

Vi ses! – Goodbye!

Glossary

cereals Grain crops such as wheat, barley, maize and rye.

dairy farming Keeping cows to make use of their milk.

handball A game where goals are scored in a net like football, but players use their hands and a small ball.

kalaha A board game that's popular in Scandinavia. It is based on an old African game played with pebbles on a pitted wooden board.

rye bread A dark, heavy bread made from rye flour instead of wheat flour.

Scandinavia A region in northern Europe that usually includes Denmark, Norway, Sweden and Iceland. Finland is sometimes considered part of Scandinavia too.

smørrebrød A Danish open sandwich made from rye bread with various toppings.

Index